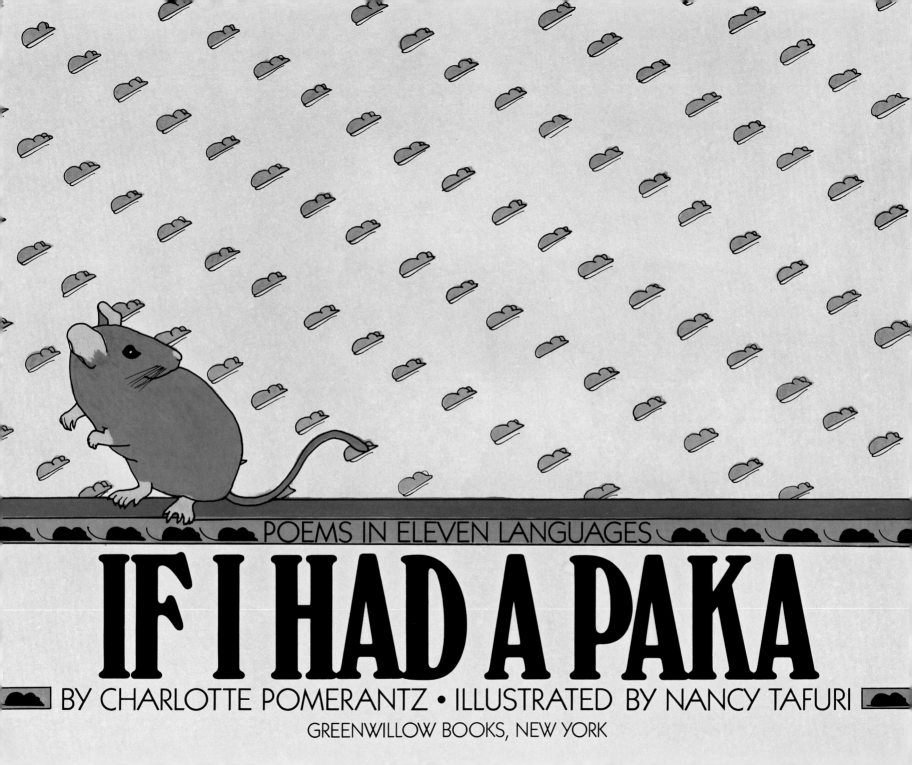

POEMS IN ELEVEN LANGUAGES

IF I HAD A PAKA

BY CHARLOTTE POMERANTZ · ILLUSTRATED BY NANCY TAFURI

GREENWILLOW BOOKS, NEW YORK

Watercolor paints and a black pen
were used for the full-color art.
The text type is ITC Kabel Medium.

Text copyright © 1982 by Charlotte Pomerantz
Illustrations copyright © 1982 by Nancy Tafuri
First published in 1982 by Greenwillow Books;
reissued in 1993.
Printed in Singapore by Tien Wah Press
First Edition
10 9 8 7 6 5 4 3 2 1

The Library of Congress cataloged an earlier issue
of this title as follows:

Pomerantz, Charlotte.
If I had a paka.
Summary: A collection of twelve poems using
eleven languages, including "If I Had a Paka"
with Swahili words; "Lulu, Lulu, I've a Lilo"
with Samoan words; and others.
1. Children's poetry, American.
[1. American poetry. 2. Languages,
Modern—Vocabulary—Poetry]
I. Tafuri, Nancy, ill. II. Title.
PS3566.0538133   811'.54   81-6624
ISBN 0-688-00836-4   AACR2
ISBN 0-688-00837-2 (lib. bdg.)

New edition:
ISBN 0-688-11900-X (trade).
ISBN 0-688-11901-8 (lib. bdg.)

For my mother and father —C. P.

For Cristina —N. T.

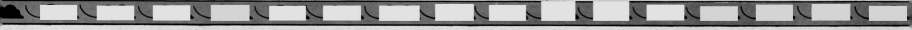

SWAHILI
IF I HAD A PAKA

If I had a paka—
meow, meow,
meow, meow—

I would want a mm-bwa—
bow wow wow wow.
If I had a mm-bwa—
bow wow wow wow—

I would want a simba—
roar, roar, roar, roar.
If I had a simba—
roar, roar, roar, roar—

I would want a jo<u>go</u>—
cockadoodle-doodle-doo.
If I had a jo<u>go</u>—
cockadoodle-doodle-doo—

I would want a poonda—
hee-haw, hee-haw.
If I had a poonda—
hee-haw, hee-haw—

I would want a kon<u>do</u>—
bah bah bah bah.
If I had a kon<u>do</u>—
bah bah bah bah—

I'd want a rafeeki—
good friend, true friend.
Had I a rafeeki—
one good true friend—
I would be content.

THE KING OF MAGLA AND VLAGA

"I am the King of Magla and Vlaga.
The King of Fog and Mist.
Look for me in the magla and vlaga,
For I have never been kissed."

"I am the Queen of Vetar and Sunce.
The Queen of Wind and Sun.
I'll look for you in the magla and vlaga,
For I can find anyone."

In vetar and sunce the Queen came down,
And beheld the King's misty charms.
She fixed her gaze on his cool pale lips
And reached out her golden arms.

"I love you," she said. "And I, you," said the King.
"But I beg you, do not come near.
For if wind and sun touch fog and mist,
Alas, I will disappear."

In sorrow the Queen left the magla and vlaga,
Returning in haste to the sky.
But she did not forget the misty-eyed King,
And at sunset she heard him sigh:

"I am the King of Magla and Vlaga.
The King of Fog and Mist.
The Queen of Vetar and Sunce once loved me.
And once I was almost kissed."

NATIVE AMERICAN

WHERE DO THESE WORDS COME FROM?

Hominy, succotash, raccoon, moose.
Succotash, raccoon, moose, papoose.

Raccoon, moose, papoose, squash, skunk.
Moose, papoose, squash, skunk, chipmunk.

Papoose, squash, skunk, chipmunk, muckamuck.
Skunk, chipmunk, muckamuck, woodchuck.

ENGLISH
YOU TAKE THE BLUEBERRY

You take the blueberry.
I'll take the dewberry.
You don't want the blueberry?
O.K. Take the bayberry.
I'll take the blueberry.

You take the bayberry.
I'll take the dayberry.
You don't want the bayberry?
O.K. Take the snowberry.
I'll take the bayberry.

You take the snowberry.
I'll take the crowberry.
You don't want the snowberry?
O.K. Take the tangleberry.
I'll take the snowberry.

You take the tangleberry.
I'll take the dangleberry.
You don't want the tangleberry?
O.K. Take the thimbleberry.
I'll take the tangleberry.

You take the thimbleberry.
I'll take the bumbleberry.
You don't want the thimbleberry?
O.K. Take the huckleberry.
I'll take the thimbleberry.

You take the huckleberry.
I'll take the chuckleberry.
You don't want the huckleberry?
O.K. Take the chuckleberry.

Chuckle, chuckle, chuckleberry.
Chuckle, I am very merry.
Ha! There is no chuckleberry.
I made up the chuckleberry.
And because you're spoiled, very,
Ha! I ate the huckleberry.
Sweet as honeysuckle berry.
Poor you, what bad luckleberry.

SAMOAN
LULU, LULU, I'VE A LILO'

Owl, owl,
I've a secret.
And I am to blame.
I lost my brand-new handkerchief.
Isn't that a shame?
But you can't tell my secret, owl.
You don't know my name.

Lulu, lulu,
I've a lilo.
And I am to blame.
I lost my brand-new solosolo.
Isn't that a shame?
But you can't tell my lilo, lulu.
You don't know my name.

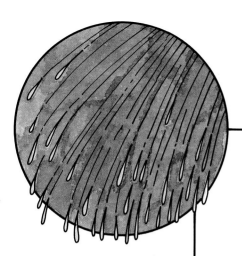

SERBO-CROATIAN
YES, IT'S RAINING

Pada kiša.*
> Yes, it's raining.

Pada sneg.
> Yes, it's snowing.

Have a cup of Turkish coffee.
> Turska kafa? I should like that.
> But I must be going.

Munja? Grom?
> Yes, lightning, thunder.

Vetar duva?
> Yes, winds blowing.

Have a cup of Turkish coffee.
> Turska kafa? How I love it.
> But I must be going.

Smell it brewing in the pot,
Thick and black and sweet and hot.
Have a cup of Turska kafa.
> No, no, no, I must be going.
> Then again—why not?

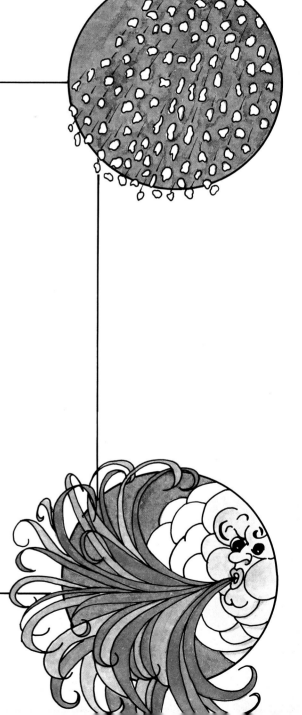

*pronounced keesha

Birch

Breadfruit

DUTCH TREES

Berkeboom

Broodboom

Kokos, kokos, klapperboom

Tulpeboom

Amandelboom

Mango, mango, mangoboom

Coconut

Tulip

Kalebassen

bassen

bassen

Kalebassen

bassen—

Boom!

Birch tree

Breadfruit tree

Coconut, coconut, coconut tree

Tulip tree

Almond tree

Mango, mango, mango tree

Calabashes

bashes

bashes

Calabashes

bashes—

Tree!

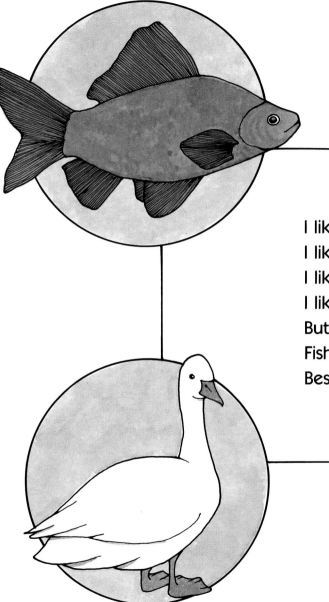

VIETNAMESE
TOY TIK KA

I like fish. Toy tik ka.
I like chicken. Toy tik ga.
I like duck. Toy tik veet.
I like meat. Toy tik teet.
But though I like ka, ga, veet, teet—
Fish and chicken, duck and meat—
Best of all I like to eat.

JAPANESE
A HIKOKA IN A HIKOKI

Whenever someone asks me what I want to be,
I answer a hikoka in a hikoki:
A pilot in an airplane—brave, alone and free.
Unless, of course, I chanced to meet another kid, and she,
Whenever someone asked her what she would like to be,
Answered a hikoka in a hikoki.
In which case—oh, what fun!—she could fly the plane with me.

INDONESIAN
DOOR NUMBER FOUR

Above my uncle's grocery store
is a pintu,
is a door.
On the pintu
is a number,
nomer empat,
number four.
In the door
there is a key.
Turn it,
enter quietly.
Hush hush, diam-diam,
quietly.
There, in lamplight,
you will see
a friend,
teman,
a friend
who's me.

SPANISH
RICE AND BEANS—
ARROZ Y HABICHUELAS

I like arroz y habichuelas.
I'm not at all fond of beans and rice.
Grandma isn't like other abuelas.
She gives me arroz y habichuelas.
Other abuelas, not half so nice,
Are always giving me beans and rice.

YIDDISH
LULLABY

Shlof, sleep through the night.
You will awake big and strong.
For your grandma, dein bubba, is right,
Except when dein bubba is wrong.